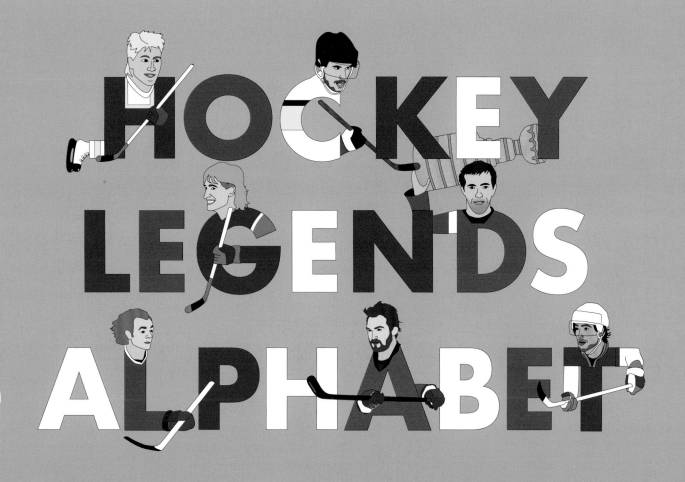

HOCKEY LEGENDS ALPHABET

Words by Robin Feiner

A is for **A**lexander Ovechkin. Thanks to his lightning speed, laser shot and undying motor, 'Ovi' became the second-youngest player to score 700 goals. When he led the Washington Capitals to their first Stanley Cup title in 2018, his wild celebrations became just as legendary as his play.

B is for Martin **B**rodeur.
The backbone of a dominant
New Jersey Devils defense,
Brodeur holds career records
in wins, shutouts and games
played. He broke the mold
with his aggressive, creative
play, leaving his crease to
play the puck and dictate
the action.

C is for Sidney **C**rosby. 'Sid the Kid' is the best player of his generation, using unparalleled vision, faceoff mastery and sheer will to "create a mountain of hockey excellence." He has led the Pittsburgh Penguins to multiple Stanley Cups, and Canada to two Olympic gold medals.

D is for Pavel Datsyuk. A magician with the puck, he wowed fans with otherworldly shootout goals and 'Datsyukian' dekes, passes and tricks. Also one of the best defensive forwards ever, the center worked tirelessly to win two Stanley Cups during his 14-season Detroit Red Wings career.

E is for Phil Esposito. Esposito terrorized opponents by being a nightmare in front of the net. The Bruins superstar led the NHL in goals for six straight seasons from 1969-75, stuffing in rebounds by the dozens. Bumper stickers around Boston read, "Jesus saves ... and Espo scores on the rebound."

F is for Grant **F**uhr.
Breaking new ground in
the sport, Fuhr was the first
black player inducted into
the Hockey Hall of Fame.
He became legendary for the
hybrid style of goaltending
that led to five Stanley Cup
wins with the Edmonton
Oilers in the 1980s.

G is for Gordie Howe. After a five-decade long career, 'Mr. Hockey' retired at age 52 with records for career games, goals and assists. No wonder he was Wayne Gretzky's idol! Mixing legendary offense with hard-nosed toughness, he wowed with his 'Gordie Howe hat trick' – a goal, assist and fight in the same game!

H is for Brett **H**ull.
A rock star on and off the ice, 'The Golden Brett' had a supernatural scoring ability despite being the focal point of opposing defenses. The St. Louis Blues legend retired with 741 career goals, third-most at the time.

Ii

I is for Jarome Iginla. Iginla broke ground by becoming the first black man to win Olympic gold when Canada prevailed at the 2002 Winter Games. Scoring 625 career goals, 'Iggy' is a Calgary Flames fan favorite, and his No. 12 was retired by the team in 2019.

J is for Jaromír Jágr. The flowing mullet. The freakish skill. The undying passion. Jágr, who retired second in career points, formed a lethal partnership with mentor and fellow Penguins legend Mario Lemieux. It's fitting that the letters of 'Jaromír' can be rearranged to spell 'Mario Jr.'

K is for **K**en Dryden. Packing plenty into his eight-season career with the Montreal Canadiens, the 'four-story goalie' won six Stanley Cups and five Vezina Trophies. And his brilliance continued beyond the crease – Dryden also held a law degree and was a Member of Parliament after his playing days.

L is for Guy Lafleur.
One of the crown jewels
of the NHL's superstar team,
'The Flower' dazzled with
charismatic creativity and
ingenious improvization.
The Montreal Canadiens
forward was the first to score
at least 50 goals and 100
points in six straight seasons.

Mm

M is for **M**ark Messier.
One of hockey's most
legendary leaders, Messier
was the first to captain two
teams – the Edmonton Oilers
and New York Rangers –
to the Stanley Cup title.
With his punishing physicality,
intense gaze and wicked wrist
shot, he intimidated and
dominated for 25 seasons.

N is for Scott **N**iedermayer. A defensive stalwart for the New Jersey Devils and Anaheim Ducks, Niedermayer's smooth skating and unflappable nature made him a perfect defensive anchor. As comfortable rushing up the ice as he was locking down top scorers, he lifted the Stanley Cup four times.

O is for Bobby Orr.
The gold standard for defensemen with eight consecutive Norris Trophy wins, Orr revolutionized his position by controlling games from all over the ice. The Boston Bruins legend awed crowds with his end-to-end rushes, spinning and darting through defenders with speed and grace.

P is for **P**atrick Roy. His quirky, theatrical play and unmistakable butterfly goaltending style made 'Saint Patrick' truly unique. Playing his best when it mattered most, Roy won two Stanley Cups each with the Montreal Canadiens and Colorado Avalanche, and retired with records for playoff shutouts and wins.

Q is for Bill Quackenbush. Relying more on his brains than his brawn, 'Quack' used efficient movement and genius positioning to become the top defenseman of the 1940s and '50s. His astounding 131 consecutive games without a penalty from 1948 – 50 is unheard of for defenders of any era.

R is for Maurice Richard. A cultural icon in French Canadian history, 'Rocket' was one of the most intense and feared players of his generation. The turbocharged forward won eight Stanley Cups in 18 seasons with the Montreal Canadiens! The Maurice Richard Trophy is now given to the NHL's top goalscorer each season.

S is for Terry Sawchuk. Playing through incredible pain during his career, Sawchuk won four Vezina Trophies and four Stanley Cups. The goaltender's crouching style changed the way the position was played, providing a better line of vision for picking up the puck.

T is for **T**eemu Selänne. With lightning speed, 'The Finnish Flash' zoomed in from the right-wing time after time on his way to 684 career goals. The excitement machine's positive attitude and offensive bursts were as enchanting as his fan interactions.

U is for Norm **U**llman. Ullman was a model of consistency, always doing the dirty work on the forecheck and in the corners. He often lined up next to flashier superstars, but that didn't stop him from being an 11-time All Star and Hall of Fame inductee.

V is for Georges **V**ézina. Standing tall, the 'Chicoutimi Cucumber' exuded quiet confidence on and off the ice. From his 1910 debut, before the NHL existed, until his 1925 retirement, nobody else played in the Montreal Canadiens net. The Vezina Trophy is now given to the NHL's best goalie each season.

W is for Wayne Gretzky. 'The Great One' is undoubtedly the best to ever lace up skates. Wearing his legendary, now-retired No. 99, the wiry Gretzky masterfully controlled games with his stick, vision and intelligence, notching up a record 894 goals and 1,963 assists.

X is for **Mario Lemieux.** Arguably the most naturally gifted player ever, 'Super Mario' was a silky-smooth skater and puck-handling wizard who overcame injury and illness to score 690 career goals. A Pittsburgh Penguins icon, Lemieux saved the franchise as both a player and an owner.

Yy

Y is for Steve Yzerman. 'Stevie Y' was a beloved leader and never-say-die competitor with an unquenchable thirst for winning. Transforming the Detroit Red Wings from perennial losers to powerhouse leaders, he drove the team to three Stanley Cups before retiring sixth in career points.

Z is for **Z**deno Chára.
A giant on the ice, Chára's
6'9'' frame set a mark for
the NHL's tallest player.
'Big Z' puts his entire weight
behind his bone-rattling
checks and record-setting
slap shot. The legendary
defenseman captained
the Boston Bruins to the
2011 Stanley Cup title.

The ever-expanding legendary library

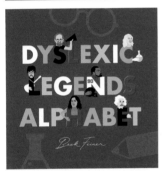 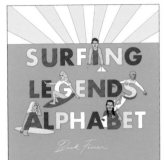 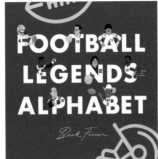 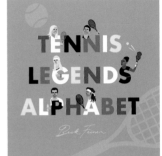        

EXPLORE THESE LEGENDARY ALPHABETS & MORE AT WWW.ALPHABETLEGENDS.COM

HOCKEY LEGENDS ALPHABET
www.alphabetlegends.com

Published by Alphabet Legends Pty Ltd in 2020
Created by Beck Feiner
Copyright © Alphabet Legends Pty Ltd 2020

978-0-6486724-3-2

Stats as at July 2020.

Printed and bound in China.